AMERICAN DEBATES AND SPEECHES

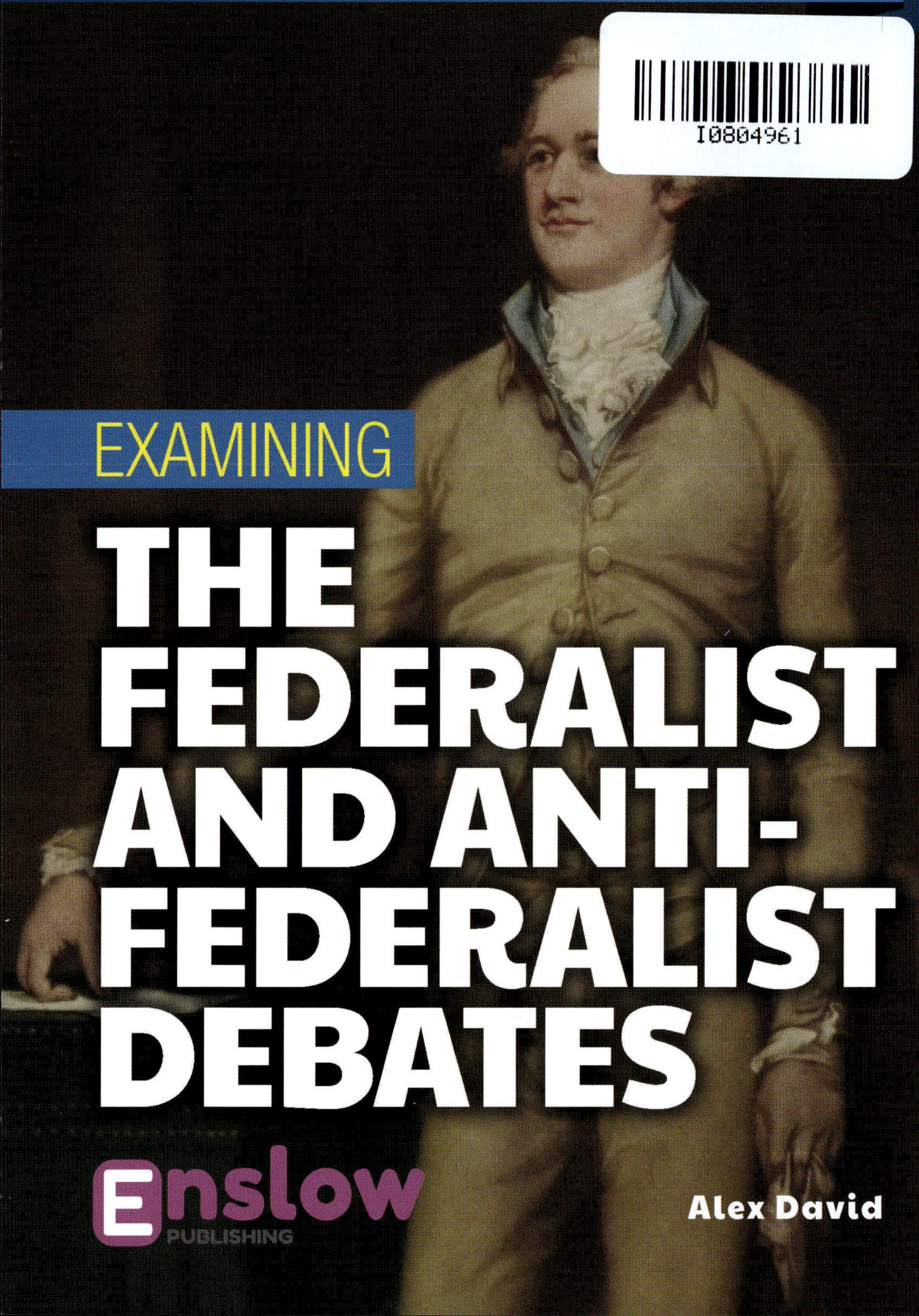

EXAMINING

THE FEDERALIST AND ANTI-FEDERALIST DEBATES

Enslow PUBLISHING

Alex David

Published in 2021 by Enslow Publishing, LLC
101 W. 23rd Street, Suite 240, New York, NY 10011

Cataloging-in-Publication Data
Names: David, Alex.
Title: Examining the federalist and anti-federalist debates / Alex David.
Description: New York : Enslow Publishing, 2021. | Series: American debates and speeches | Includes glossary and index.
Identifiers: ISBN 9781978515123 (pbk.) | ISBN 9781978515130 (library bound)
Subjects: LCSH: Federalist--Juvenile literature. | Constitutional history--United States--Juvenile literature. | Federal government--United States--History--18th century--Juvenile literature. United States--Politics and government--1783-1789--Juvenile literature.
Classification: LCC KF4515.D38 2020 | DDC 342.7302'4--dc23

Printed in the United States of America

To Our Readers: We have done our best to make sure all websites in this book were active and appropriate when we went to press. However, the author and the publisher have no control over and assume no liability for the material available on those websites or on any websites they may link to. Any comments or suggestions can be sent by email to customerservice@enslow.com.

Photos Credits: Photo research by Bruce Donnola
Cover, pp. 1, 21 Library of Congress Prints and Photographs Division; p. 5 Interfoto/Alamy Stock Photo; p. 8 GraphicaArtis/Hulton Archive/Getty Images; p. 9 Smith Collection/Gado/Archive Photos/Getty Images; p. 13 Hulton Archive/Archive Photos/Getty Images; p. 17 New York Public Library, USA/Bridgeman Images; p. 19 National Gallery Of Art/The LIFE Picture Collection/ Getty Images; pp. 20, 42 Universal History Archive/Universal Images Group/Getty Images; p. 23 Stock Montage/Archive Photos/Getty Images; p. 24 The Picture Art Collection/Alamy Stock Photo; p. 27 Fotosearch/Archive Photos/Getty Images; p. 30 travelview/Shutterstock.com; pp. 33, 40 MPI/Archive Photos/Getty Images; p. 36 Lawrence Thornton/Archive Photos/Getty Images; p. 38 Universal Images Group North America LLC/Alamy Stock Photo; p. 44 Heritage Images/Hulton Fine Art Collection/Getty Images; p. 45 Stock Montage/Archive Photos/Getty Images; p. 50 NurPhoto/Getty Images; Ozz Design/Shutterstock.com (back cover and interior pages background pattern); pashabo/Shutterstock.com (interior pages American flag patterns); Midwaves/Shutterstock.com, Leonid Zarubin/Shutterstock.com (interior pages abstract textures and patterns)

Portions of this book originally appeared in *The Federalist-Anti-Federalist Debate Over States' Rights* by Lea Bell.

CONTENTS

INTRODUCTION

In 1787, the writers of the Federalist Papers worried that their letters would be secretly read by postal carriers and information would be given to the Anti-Federalists. They were not wrong to fear espionage. The American Revolution had ended four years earlier, and now a new war had started. Only this war did not require muskets or cannons. Instead, it was a war of words.

Alexander Hamilton, James Madison, and John Jay, under the pen name Publius, wrote an article in the newspaper urging people to accept the new constitution. The Anti-Federalists read it and reacted, writing their own article suspicious of a government with too much power. So began a heated political debate based on reason. On the Federalist side of the debate, over 175,000 words were written over the course of seven months.

What was once "the American experiment" was now an official, independent country, the United States of America. In 1777, the Articles of Confederation had been drawn up. However, the founders of the country began to question if the Articles of Confederation were strong enough. In 1787, at the Philadelphia Constitutional Convention, a constitution had been proposed as a replacement of the Articles of Confederation. Previously, the thirteen colonies had become states when they agreed to the Declaration of Independence, but now a question remained: How would power be divided

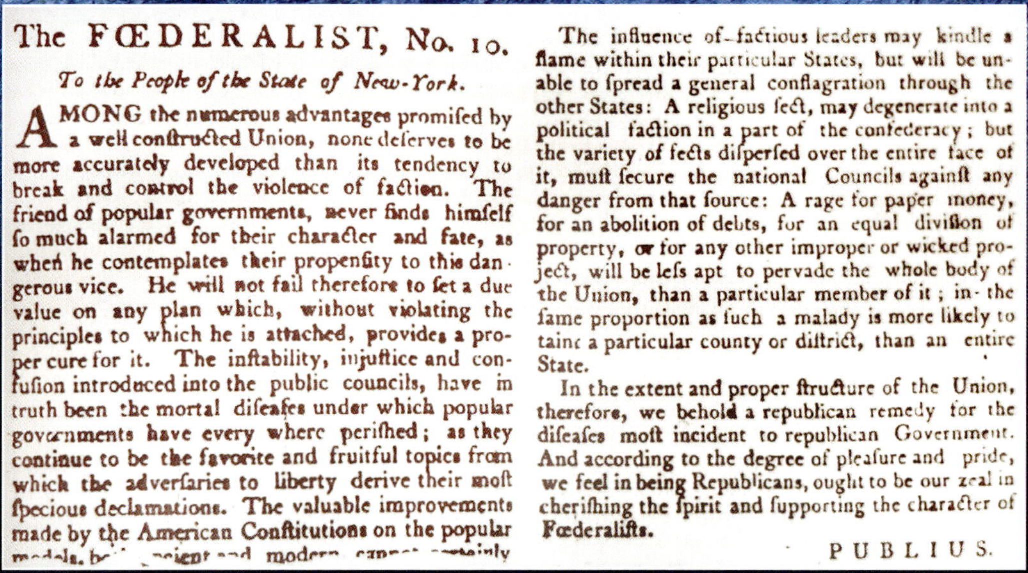

The FŒDERALIST, No. 10.

To the People of the State of New-York.

AMONG the numerous advantages promiſed by a well conſtructed Union, none deſerves to be more accurately developed than its tendency to break and control the violence of faction. The friend of popular governments, never finds himſelf ſo much alarmed for their character and fate, as when he contemplates their propenſity to this dangerous vice. He will not fail therefore to ſet a due value on any plan which, without violating the principles to which he is attached, provides a proper cure for it. The inſtability, injuſtice and confuſion introduced into the public councils, have in truth been the mortal diſeaſes under which popular governments have every where periſhed; as they continue to be the favorite and fruitful topics from which the adverſaries to liberty derive their moſt ſpecious declamations. The valuable improvements made by the American Conſtitutions on the popular [illegible]

The influence of factious leaders may kindle a flame within their particular States, but will be unable to ſpread a general conflagration through the other States: A religious ſect, may degenerate into a political faction in a part of the confederacy; but the variety of ſects diſperſed over the entire face of it, muſt ſecure the national Councils againſt any danger from that ſource: A rage for paper money, for an abolition of debts, for an equal diviſion of property, or for any other improper or wicked project, will be leſs apt to pervade the whole body of the Union, than a particular member of it; in the ſame proportion as ſuch a malady is more likely to taint a particular county or diſtrict, than an entire State.

In the extent and proper ſtructure of the Union, therefore, we behold a republican remedy for the diſeaſes moſt incident to republican Government. And according to the degree of pleaſure and pride, we feel in being Republicans, ought to be our zeal in cheriſhing the ſpirit and ſupporting the character of Fœderaliſts.

PUBLIUS.

The Federalist Papers were written using the pseudonym "Publius," as shown here, so the writers could remain anonymous.

among the new states? Would state governments have more control than the federal government? Would people value liberty or safety? The Federalist and Anti-Federalist Papers were a reasoned response to these questions.

The public read each side with eager enthusiasm. How would this new country decide how to govern itself? There was no longer a king and liberty was a large aspect of the American Revolution. But, some people wondered if there was such a thing as too much liberty.

Alexander Hamilton, of the Federalist side, thought so. He was deeply afraid of people having too much power. What if there were anarchy? He wanted a government that made its laws clear. Madison agreed with him. In Federalist Paper

Number 29, he argued "a people ought to be controlled and regulated by the government." However, Anti-Federalist, New York governor, George Clinton, writing under the pen name Cato, criticized the Constitution, this new American document. The original Constitution did not have a bill of rights and it was largely due to the Anti-Federalists that we have the Bill of Rights today.

To understand the Federalist and Anti-Federalist Papers is to understand the reasons behind the US Constitution. Reading the pages is like listening in to the private thoughts of great intellectual minds who were deciding the intentions of a new country. Even today, many disputes that you read in the newspapers or listen to on the radio are asking some of the same essential questions of the Federalist and Anti-Federalist Papers. How much control is too much control? What is our definition of liberty? Who should have the power to control people, the national government or state governments? In the years after this debate, America fought the Civil War which was largely about the role of slavery in America as well as states' rights. It is perhaps in the nature of the American identity to question our liberties. Freedom has been a founding principle and yet, the Federalists won the argument. They decided that liberty needed to have restraint. America didn't want a king, or an authoritarian tyrant, but it needed order. As you will read, the debate to get to this conclusion is an exciting and complicated one.

CHAPTER ONE

NEW RULES FOR A NEW COUNTRY

The late 1700s were an exciting time for Americans. The revolution had ended and America was at last free from the oppression of the British government. During the revolution, colonists had stitched "Give me Liberty or Give me Death" on their uniforms, and now they had liberty, but what would this new country do with all the freedom?

A new government would have to be formed. Philosophical questions about the nature of humans would have to be answered. If given freedom, would people still act generously and fairly or would they act only with self-interest? Using the British constitution and system of government as their template—both to react against and to emulate—early American thinkers needed a document that would set the intentions for this vast, new country.

First Official Constitution

It did not take long before issues began to pop up that proved to people that some kind of government was needed within

Colonial Americans were curious about the news of their new country and would listen to town criers read the news.

the thirteen states. In 1777, a document called the Articles of Confederation was drafted. Four years later, it was ratified. As the first official constitution of the United States, it was the main set of rules and regulations that guided the new states through their first few years.

Deciding what would go into this first constitution was not an easy process. Every decision seemed to require long, detailed debates. In the end, the Articles of Confederation established a permanent national congress, made up of two to seven delegates from each of the thirteen states. There

To all to whom these Presents shall come we the undersigned Delegates of the States affixed to our Names send greeting. Whereas the Delegates of the United States of America in Congress assembled did on the fifteenth day of November in the Year of our Lord One Thousand Seven Hundred and Seventy seven, and in the Second Year of the Independence of America agree to certain articles of Confederation and perpetual Union between the States of Newhampshire, Massachusetts-bay, Rhode-island and Providence Plantations, Connecticut, New York, New Jersey, Pennsylvania, Delaware, Maryland, Virginia, North Carolina, South Carolina and Georgia in the Words following, viz. "Articles of Confederation and perpetual Union between the states of Newhampshire, Massachusetts-bay, Rhodeisland and Providence Plantations, Connecticut, New-York, New-Jersey, Pennsylvania, Delaware, Maryland, Virginia, North-Carolina, South-Carolina and Georgia.

Article I. The Stile of this confederacy shall be "The United States of America."

Article II. Each state retains its sovereignty, freedom and independence, and every Power, Jurisdiction and right, which is not by this confederation expressly delegated to the United States, in Congress assembled.

Article III. The said states hereby severally enter into a firm league of friendship with each other, for their common defence, the security of their Liberties, and their mutual and general welfare, binding themselves to assist each other, against all force offered to, or attacks made upon them, or any of them, on account of religion, sovereignty, trade, or any other pretence whatever.

Article IV. The better to secure and perpetuate mutual friendship and intercourse among the people of the different states in this union, the free inhabitants of each of these states, paupers, vagabonds and fugitives from Justice excepted, shall be entitled to all privileges and immunities of free citizens in the several states; and the people of each state shall have free ingress and regress to and from any other state, and shall enjoy therein all the privileges of trade and commerce, subject to the same duties, impositions and restrictions as the inhabitants thereof respectively, provided that such restriction shall not extend so far as to prevent the removal of property imported into any state, to any other state of which the Owner is an inhabitant; provided also that no imposition, duties or restriction shall be laid by any state, on the property of the united states, or either of them.

If any Person guilty of, or charged with treason, felony, or

The Articles of Confederation is shown here.

was no executive or judicial branch yet. Congress would be empowered to declare war or peace, handle foreign relations, and keep an army and navy. Ironically, it could create laws, yet it could not enforce them. The states could simply choose whether they wanted to go along with Congress's directives.

In 1787, Congress enacted an important piece of legislation called the Northwest Ordinance. This law was established to describe exactly how new states would be formed from the various lands won in the Revolutionary War. The northwest region, the area between the Ohio and Mississippi Rivers and by the Great Lakes, was split up into territories, and governors, judges, and secretaries were appointed for each one. (The role of the secretaries was to maintain the public records.) The ordinance established that once a territory reached a population of five thousand adult men, the territory could elect a representative to Congress. When the population reached sixty thousand adult men, it could officially apply for statehood. (The number of women, non-white people, and children at that time was considered irrelevant.)

In the beginning, the Articles of Confederation was adequate for the new states. It described the relationship between the states as a "firm league of friendship." It had not, however, created a union as had been hoped. Instead, the states were considered to be connected by what George Washington referred to as "a rope of sand," in a February 28, 1785, letter to Henry Knox. In other words, the union was not very strong. It quickly became obvious that the system of governance that was laid out in the Articles of Confederation was inadequate to meet the growing needs of the new country. The individual

The Need for a Constitution

In Massachusetts in 1786, many ex-soldiers had returned to their farms. During the revolution, they received meager payment, and now the American government was asking them to pay off their farms, which they had borrowed on credit before the war. Additionally, they were being taxed higher than they had been when England was in charge.

Farmer and former Continental army captain, Daniel Shays, thought this was unfair. In September of 1786, Shays led six hundred men to Springfield, Massachusetts, to peacefully shut down the court. However, soon the peaceful protest began to turn into a violent insurrection. In 1787, Shays and two thousand of his men were captured. They were sentenced to death, but then later, they were pardoned.

Massachusetts appealed to the federal government for help, but, under the Articles of Confederation, the government was powerless to act. The event made many believe that the Articles of Confederation was too weak a document. It helped Alexander Hamilton make the argument for a document which allowed the federal government to have more power than individual states.

states began to demand changes, and slowly the document began to be watered down with various revisions and amendments. Something more structured and extensive was needed.

A Nation Outgrows the Articles

In 1786, a group of businessmen met in Annapolis, Maryland, to talk about some problems they had been having with commerce that involved people in different states. As they discussed the issues, they began to realize that business was only the beginning of the problems. It was obvious that the new nation was outgrowing the Articles of Confederation. It seemed like each person had a question or issue that was not covered by the articles, and so they were not sure what to do about it. Finally, they decided to hold a convention to explore either a complete revision of the articles or the creation of a similar document that had a wider scope.

The Constitutional Convention

In May 1787, a group of delegates gathered in Philadelphia once again to take a slow, careful, and thoughtful look at the Articles of Confederation and to decide what was needed. They wanted to find a way to unite the thirteen states. George Washington was elected president of what was called the Constitutional Convention. His diplomatic skills were well known and would be well tested during this event. Many different plans and ideas were suggested, some with great heat and passion. However, the delegates generally realized that the occasion called for calm and tact to keep it under control as everything was suggested, discussed, and then either accepted or rejected.

George Washington, illustrated here, speaks at the Constitutional Convention in 1787.

Possible Plans

The Virginia Plan, for instance, proposed that the country have a bicameral (two-house) legislature. It also suggested that a state's representation in the federal government should be based on the population or wealth of the state. This was upsetting to delegates from the smaller states, who feared that this arrangement would not give them the level of representation they wanted. The New Jersey Plan made another suggestion: states would have equal representation, but there would be a Supreme Court. Connecticut suggested the final compromise between the plans. The country would have a bicameral legislature. The upper house would be the Senate. In it, each state would have equal representation. The lower house would be the House of Representatives. There, representation would be based on the population of the state. The new government would also have a Supreme Court and a complex system of checks and balances built into it. This would ensure that no one branch of government would have too much power. For every power granted to one branch of government, the others would have the ability to stop or check it.

Bundle of Compromises

Putting together the actual Constitution of the United States was an incredibly complicated procedure. Arguments emerged constantly, and educated and dedicated men debated issue after issue. It slowly came together, incorporating many different ideas, until some people began to refer to it as a "bundle of compromises." Finally, the document was completed, and it was time for the next big step: ratification. Nine of the thirteen states had to approve the new Constitution before it could become official. It was a procedure that took three years to accomplish. While some states—like Delaware, New Jersey, and Georgia—agreed almost immediately, other states were slower to respond. Certain issues were still being debated. As more people began to speak out against various provisions of the new document, strong advocates of the Constitution began to worry. The country seemed equally divided between those who agreed and those who disagreed with the Constitution.

Four weeks after the Constitution was presented for ratification, an essay explaining why all the states should approve it appeared in the *Independent Journal*. It focused on the document's integrity. Shortly after, a rebuttal appeared—and a new form of national debate was born. In print, essay by essay, week by week, the two political groups that would come to be known as the Federalists and the Anti-Federalists shared their hopes, worries, thoughts, and comments about the future of the nation.

CHAPTER TWO

THE DEBATERS

For seven months, the Federalists and the Anti-Federalists engaged in a heated debate. Newspapers like New York's *Independent Journal* and *Poughkeepsie Country Journal*, Philadelphia's *Freeman's Journal,* and Boston's *American Herald* would publish each side's argument, sometimes one or two essays appearing per week. Rhetoric was used and at times the essays appeared propagandistic. The writers swore themselves to secrecy and even years after the Constitution was ratified, the writers did not reveal themselves.

In 1788, the Federalist essays were published in a book under the pseudonym Publius. It wasn't until 1792, in a French edition, that Hamilton, Madison, and Jay were revealed as the writers of the work. The French were so impressed by these thinkers they offered honorary citizenship to Hamilton and Madison.

So, why did they write under pen names?

First, in the 1700s, it was common for writers to write using a pseudonym. Second, if readers knew the true identity of the writers, they would ascribe everything they knew about the person to their argument. For instance, Madison was from

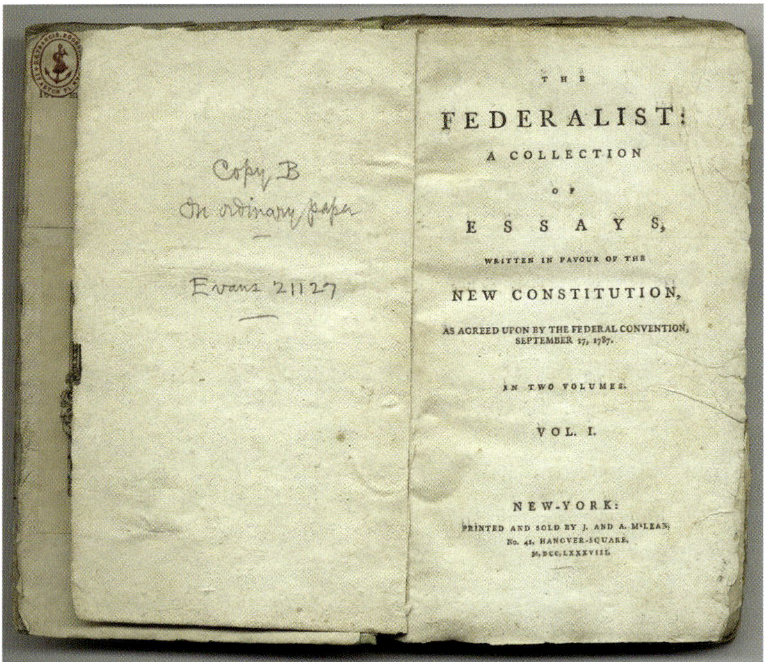

In 1788, all of the Federalist essays were collected and published in a book called *The Federalist*.

the South and he owned a plantation. Hamilton was from the North and often aligned himself with the identity and interest of his state: New York. By combining identities, the writers were able to fuse these two, very separate viewpoints into one character. Publius became his own character, and some historians argue it was America's first fictitious character. Someone readers could align with or imagine him, much like Rip van Winkle or Huck Finn. Both sides used pen names and although there continues to be discrepancy about who wrote what essay, we now know who each writer really was.

Hamilton, Madison, and Jay: The Federalists

Without a doubt, between the two political groups, the Federalists were more organized and effective in presenting their side of the debate. Their eighty-five essays were quite orderly, and although there were three primary writers, Alexander Hamilton, James Madison, and John Jay, each one attempted to imitate the others' style so as to appear as one writer. Although it has not been proven, historians suspect the men read each other's work and discussed what needed to be written next.

Hamilton, Madison, and Jay created the persona Publius. They chose this name because of a Roman statesman named Publius Valerius Publicola. Hamilton and the others chose this name because the real Publius warned Roman citizens of threats to their freedom.

Alexander Hamilton

The first person to develop the idea of a series of newspaper articles supporting the ratification of the Constitution was Alexander Hamilton. A former special aide and personal friend to George Washington, he already had a great deal of experience as a writer of newspaper essays and pamphlets. Hamilton represented New York at the convention in Annapolis and was one of the people responsible for arranging the ensuing Constitutional Convention.

Hamilton wanted to see a strong central government in place in the United States. He felt that ratification of the new

Constitution was the primary way to achieve that. He was a strong believer in organization and order and feared that if the Constitution was not adopted, the new nation would see complete lawlessness. Businessmen supported Hamilton because he encouraged the ideas of a large national bank and mint that supported commerce and industrial development.

Alexander Hamilton is shown above. This portrait was done around 1806 by John Trumbull.

Hamilton wanted to help ensure that the necessary nine states ratified the Constitution, so he came up with the idea of writing essays for the newspapers. He was not sure that he could do it alone, however, so he turned to some of his colleagues and asked for their help. The first person he asked for help was John Jay. In the end, Hamilton wrote fifty-one of the eighty-five Federalist essays.

John Jay

Jay had been one of the main people involved in negotiating peace with Great Britain at the end of the Revolutionary War. Under the Articles of Confederation, he was the secretary for foreign affairs. When Hamilton asked him to write some essays about foreign policy for the newspapers, he agreed. Because of poor health, he wrote only five essays. However, they were important ones. They dealt primarily with the international advantages of adopting the Constitution.

John Jay, painted above, was the first Chief Justice of the United States.

Next, Hamilton asked Gouverneur Morris to join the Federalist team, but he declined. He had a strong background in law, and the 173 speeches he had made during the Constitutional Convention had made a strong impression on Hamilton. Morris was one of the main people to draft the Constitution. Hamilton had hoped he would add his prolific thoughts to the series of essays. However, Morris was deeply involved in his business and could not spare the time.

A man named William Duer was asked to join the Federalists. He was the assistant secretary to Hamilton at the time. He submitted three essays for the Federalists. Hamilton rejected each one and was forced to find one more writer. This time he selected James Madison, a future president of the United States.

James Madison

Madison was sometimes called the father of the Constitution because of the dedication and faith he put into it. Although George Washington was elected president of the Constitutional Convention, it was actually Madison who acted as primary leader. He accepted the Federalists' offer and ended up writing twenty-six essays. He also co-wrote three essays with Hamilton. This was not an easy process since the two men did not always see eye to eye on some issues, even though they were both Federalists.

James Madison is pictured above. He wrote the Federalist essays with Hamilton and Jay under the name "Publius."

The Anti-Federalist Writers

The Anti-Federalists were not as structured as their opponents. However, they were just as passionate about their beliefs. Instead of multiple writers using one pen name, each person took his own pseudonym. Although their leader was often considered to be Thomas Jefferson, he did not write any of the Anti-Federalist essays.

Samuel Bryan as Centinel

The most prolific of the Anti-Federalist writers was Centinel. He wrote a total of twenty-four essays between October 1787 and November 1788. Most of these were published in Philadelphia newspapers. His main focus was on the

An Unlikely Friendship

John Jay was quite sick when the Federalist Papers were being written, so he only wrote five of them. It was up to Madison and Hamilton to write the rest. Hamilton wrote 51 and Madison wrote 29 of the essays.

Hamilton and Madison, although very different, became friends during the project. They met at the Confederation Congress in 1782 and hit it off because they both wanted the federal government to have more power than the states. However, they had very different temperaments. Although both were young men (in their thirties), Hamilton was volatile and excited, where as Madison was highly intellectual and priggish. During the project, they became close friends and campaigned together for the nation to approve ratification, However, in the years after it was completed, they parted ways. Later, Hamilton would say that his one time friend, Madison, was "his personal and political enemy."

system of checks and balances that had been built into the Constitution. Historians believe that Centinel was most likely a man named Samuel Bryan, the owner of several Philadelphia newspapers.

Thomas Jefferson, shown above, became the third president of the United States.

Robert Yates as Brutus

Another frequent writer was Brutus. His sixteen articles appeared in New York's *Independent Journal*. They were widely reprinted in other newspapers. Each one was addressed to "the Citizens of the State of New York." Brutus was probably a man named Robert Yates, a New York judge. He chose the name to honor the Roman who killed Julius Caesar. Experts believe that he also wrote under the name of Sydney.

Richard Henry Lee as The Federal Farmer

The Federal Farmer wrote thirteen essays for the Anti-Federalists. Most of them were printed in New York's *Poughkeepsie Country Journal*. He is thought to be either

Here is a portrait of Mercy Otis Warren from around 1763. She wrote under the pen name "A Columbian Patriot."

Richard Henry Lee, a delegate from Virginia, or Melancton Smith, a delegate from New York.

The Other Writers

Other writers were Cato, most likely New York governor George Clinton, and Cincinnatus, New Yorker Arthur Lee. Additional pen names used by other writers included Philanthropos, Montezuma, Candidus, Leonidas, Aristocrotis, and Republicus. Letters by "A Columbian Patriot" actually came from the pen of a woman, Mercy Warren, sister of another Anti-Federalist named James who signed his letters either Republican Federalist or Helvidius Priscus. A few authors even signed their real names, including Virginia governor Patrick Henry, Virginia colonel William Grayson, and William Penn, the founder of Pennsylvania.

Like the Federalists, the Anti-Federalists wrote more than eighty essays. When today's readers look at any of these essays, regardless of which side of the issue they come from, it is obvious that there is a great deal of repetition within them. New essays were being published as often as four times a week. Frequently, they were reprinted in a half-dozen different newspapers. It's important to remember that when both sides penned these essays, they never imagined they would be gathered together into a book and read one after another. Instead, the essays were part of an ongoing series with days and sometimes weeks between them. In some ways, they were like a sophisticated advertising campaign in which each side kept running an advertisement of sorts, with obvious repetition to help the readers—or customers—remember the important points.

CHAPTER THREE

THE FEDERALIST ARGUMENT

In 1794, well after the Federalist Papers were complete, Hamilton wrote "If it be asked, What is the most sacred duty and the greatest source of our security in a Republic? The answer would be, An inviolable respect for the constitution and Laws." This allegiance to the Constitution was fundamental to the Federalists' argument. Each state had to agree to, or ratify, the Constitution and Hamilton, Madison, and Jay took it upon themselves to show people how important a document it was. They wanted people to understand that the Constitution would unite the country. The Articles of Confederation were inadequate and weak. Federalist essays 37 through 85 show how the Constitution could help guide the United States. It would provide peace and security and help ensure that the liberty which they just fought for in the revolution was protected.

Intentions of the Constitution

Today, the Federalist Papers are considered the definitive source for scholars on the true intentions of the Constitution.

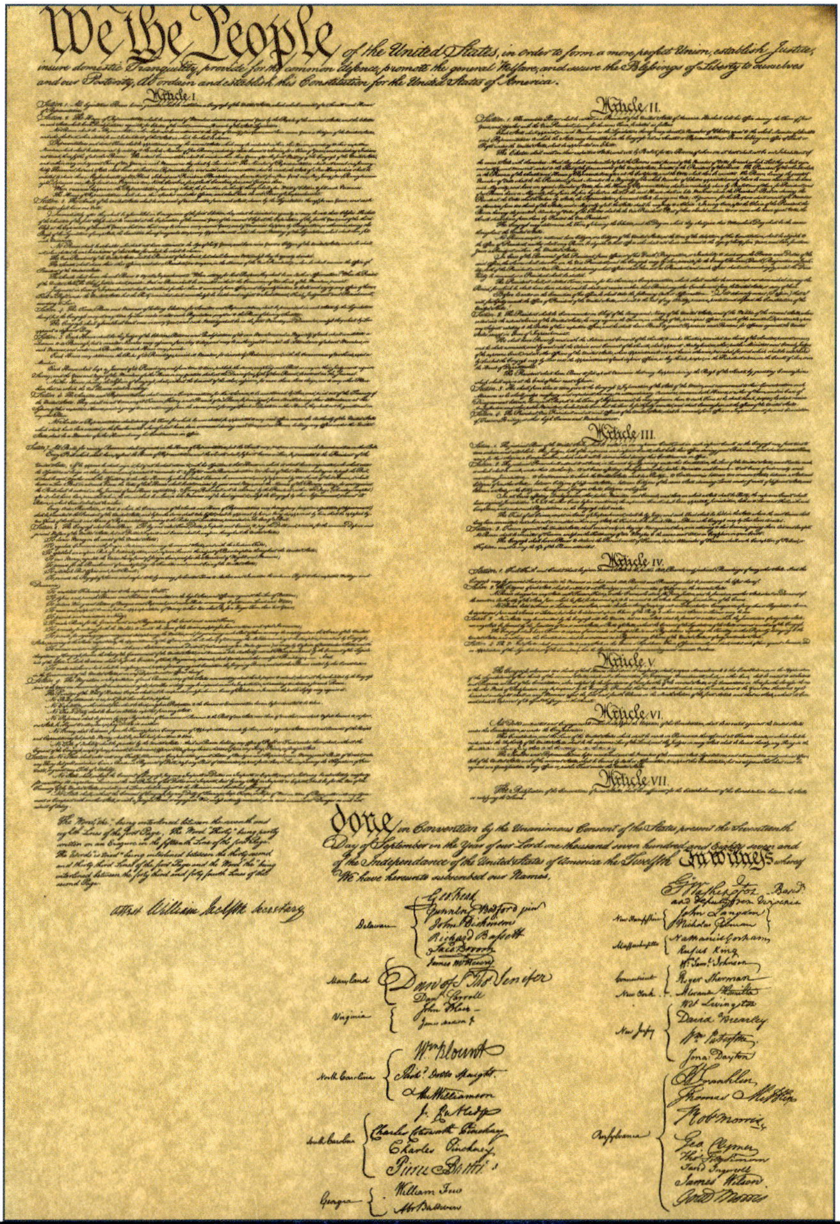

Here is a photograph of the Constitution with the signatures of delegates from each state.

Because the famous and powerful document did not provide people with any explanations and justifications for what was in it, these three men filled in the gaps. Also, through their letters to the newspapers, they told people why certain provisions had or had not been included or what changes had been made.

The Location of the Capital

As the Constitution was created, other issues pertinent to this new country had to be decided. For instance, where would the capital be?

This became an issue similar to the Federalist Papers. The framers of the Constitution wanted to make sure that the capital was a federal city, not in a state. If the capital were in a state, it would give that state an advantage. However, another challenge was where to put the capital. Should it be in the North? New York or Philadelphia seemed to make sense, but Southerners disagreed with a northern capital. Finally, it was decided that George Washington would get to decide where the capital would be located. He visited the then-barren region of the Potomac River. It was obviously much different than how Washington, DC, looks today. There were only a few streets in Georgetown. But, Washington thought that this spot was ideal for the capital. It would allow an opening to the West.

It was a marvelous and unique opportunity to sell the people on big government, one letter at a time.

18th Century Prose

The language in which the Federalist Papers were written leaves little doubt in the reader's mind that the authors were educated men. However, it also made the essays somewhat challenging for some people to understand. The English language was much more formal two hundred years ago than it is today, especially when it came to politics. Looking at the first two sentences of the "General Introduction," the first of the Federalist essays, might send many of today's readers scrambling for a dictionary. Alexander Hamilton wrote:

> After an unequivocal experience of the inefficacy of the subsisting federal government, you are called upon to deliberate on a new Constitution for the United States of America. The subject speaks its own importance: comprehending the consequences nothing less than the existence of the UNION, the safety and welfare of the parts of which it is composed, the fate of an empire in many respects the most interesting in the world.

Despite the difficult vocabulary, the "General Introduction" remains passionate and strong, more than two centuries after it was written. In it, Hamilton outlined what he had planned to do in the essays to follow. Originally, he and the other writers had estimated that there would be between twenty and

This painting is on the ceiling of the Capitol Building in Washington, DC. *E Pluribus Unum* means "From Many, One."

twenty-five pieces total. It was a surprise to them when they ended up with more than three times that amount.

First Essays

The first set of Federalist essays outlined the many ways in which the Articles of Confederation was no longer adequate for their new nation. They pointed out its weaknesses again and again, each from a slightly different angle. It was a wise way to begin their side of the debate, because most people agreed with them—the articles were no longer sufficient and needed revision. In John Jay's essays, he pointed out the similarities of the people, once again, emphasizing what everyone had in common. He listed everything from belief in the same God and use of the same language to use of the same land and the same trading system. In his second essay, he encouraged the people to use "sober consideration" instead of "blind acceptance" when it came to choosing a form of government.

From the sixth essay on, the tone changed to a more serious and demanding one. In essays 6 and 8, Hamilton wrote that he wanted a united country because he feared "frequent and violent contests" between the states otherwise. It was clear that Hamilton truly worried that, without some form of strong and powerful central government, the country would fall apart. Because he felt that the smaller states would be overtaken by the larger ones, he thought that the nation must have a standing army to prevent this situation from happening. Many of the Federalists' essays often covered the topic of states' safety over and over because it was a concern that many people shared. In essay 9, Hamilton compared the nation and the individual states with the sun and the planets that orbit around it. He used the analogy to show that just as the planets depend on the big and powerful sun for survival, so should the states revolve around a government for their survival. "A firm Union will be of the utmost moment to the peace and liberty of the states as a barrier against domestic faction and insurrection," he wrote.

The tenth essay was written by James Madison. It is considered one of the most effective of the entire series. He reminded people that establishing a government would help control the violence and damage that can be caused by factions, or people who gather to protect their own personal economic or political interests. Madison wrote:

> A zeal for different opinions concerning religion, concerning government and many other points, as well of speculation as of practice; an attachment to different leaders ambitiously contending for preeminence and power; or two persons of other descriptions whose fortunes have been interesting to the human passions, have, in turn, divided mankind into parties, inflamed them with mutual animosity and rendered them much more disposed to vex and oppress each other than to cooperate for their common good.

Essays 15 and 16 changed the tone of the papers once more. National safety was put aside, and Hamilton focused again on the "insufficiency of present confederation to the preservation of the union." He painted a rather dire picture of the country, bringing up sensitive issues such as its large debts incurred during the war, its low property values, its poor standing with other countries, and its lack of military and underdeveloped commercial sector. He reminded readers that the Federalists felt that government existed because men do not reliably conform to the "dictates of reason and justice." His party always felt that groups would act more responsibly and intelligently than individuals would. He referred to the Articles

This painting shows the White House, in Washington, DC, in 1807.

of Confederation as "the parent of anarchy" and returned to the issue of the need to keep harmony between the states. The government must "carry its agency to the persons of the citizens," he wrote.

Hamilton added in essay 22 that a strong central government would be the answer to the commercial problems of most companies. Without a strong central government, it was understandable that foreign governments were hesitant to do business with the United States. They feared that there would be hostility between the states, and according to Hamilton, the Articles of Confederation was considered "radically vicious and unsound." Before concluding, he turned to one other issue that the articles had not addressed—judiciary power. As he so eloquently phrased it, "Laws are a dead letter without courts to expound and define their true meaning and operation." He discussed what he called the Supreme Tribunal, or what is now known as the Supreme Court. Knowing that different courts and different judges often came up with different styles of ruling, he stated:

> To avoid the confusion which would unavoidably result from the contradictory decisions of a number of independent judicatories [judiciaries], all nations have found it necessary to establish one court paramount to the rest, possessing a general superintendence and authorized to settle and declare in the last resort a uniform rule of civil justice.

The first twenty-two Federalist essays achieved exactly what the authors had intended. They showed readers the flaws and dangers of the current government. They also set the scene for the next barrage of letters, which would show the perfect solution: ratification of the Constitution.

CHAPTER FOUR

DEFINING AMERICA

Today, we associate the term "republican" with a political party. However, a republic is simply a government which elects representatives and a president to represent the wishes of the people. In essays 23 through 36, the Federalists, after having shown how flawed the Articles of Confederation was, wanted people to support a document that would help to create a true republic. This meant there would be a separation of powers and there would be checks and balances.

In essay 37, Madison argues a tender issue: how to give people liberty while still having a government that would have authority over them. He wrote, "Energy in government is essential to that security against external and internal danger and to that prompt and salutary execution of the law, which enter into the very definition of good government. Stability in government is essential to national character. On comparing, however, these valuable ingredients with the vital principles of liberty, we must perceive at once the difficulty of mingling them in their due proportions."

In this portrait, from around 1800, James Madison works at his writing desk.

Separation of Powers

What precisely is a republican government based on, and how did the new Constitution meet those requirements? Those were the questions Madison set out to answer, beginning with essay 39. This new discussion brought in special terminology for readers. In essay 47, Madison talked about a specific element found in republican governments called "separation of powers." The Constitution called for three separate branches of government (legislative, executive, and judicial), and some people were concerned that the branches were not separate enough from each other. They also worried that the power was not evenly distributed among them. Madison understood this and even stated that too much power in one branch "is the very definition of tyranny." In essay 47, Madison told the people how each branch would work and what abilities it might have. This introduced the concept of "checks and balances" or the capability of one branch to have power over the actions of the other branches. This process stops any one branch from having too much power.

Liberty for All

Madison's essay 51 is considered to be one of the most important of all. He set out to clearly explain to people how the government would make liberty possible for everyone. He addressed the issue of class struggle and politics when he wrote, "It is of great importance in a republic not only to guard against the oppression of its rulers, but to guard one part of the society against the injustice of the other. Different

Early Senate chambers are pictured above.

interests necessarily exist in different classes of citizens . . . If a majority be united by a common interest the rights of the minority will be secure."

America Will Not Be Ruled By A King

In essays 62 and 63, Madison discussed some of the more detailed information found in the new Constitution, particularly within the Senate. He wrote about the qualification of senators, the method used to elect them, the concept of equal representation, the number of senators, and the length of their terms. In essay 70, Hamilton began discussing what character traits it takes to be a president and lead the country. The Federalists wanted to make sure people knew that the president was not going to lead America like the king had ruled England. He would not be immune from criticism, accountability, or even disciplinary action. Unlike royalty, the president would not be a sacred figure. Even today, this specific essay is read if there is any question about what powers the president does and does not have.

The Judicial Branch

In essay 78, Hamilton continued to educate the public about the details of the proposed Constitution. The judicial branch, considered to be the weakest branch, is the focus of this essay. Hamilton wrote, "A constitution is, in fact, and must be regarded by the judged, as a fundamental law." Hamilton believed that federal judges should hold their offices for life. After all, many laws are complex, and it could take years to fully understand their meaning. Essay 79 continued the same topic and discussed how judges should be compensated for their work. The Constitution states that US judges "shall at stated times receive for their services a compensation which shall not be diminished during their continuance in office."

The Last Essays

Hamilton wrote the last two essays of the Federalist Papers. In essay 84, he admitted that there were still some objections to the Constitution that he had not fully addressed. One of the main issues was the lack of a bill of rights. This was a much debated topic and one of the primary reasons several states were hesitant to agree to ratification. Hamilton attempted to show in this essay that despite the lack of an actual bill of rights, people did not need to worry that their interests were not going to be protected. He listed the six safeguards built into the Constitution, including separation of powers and checks and balances. There was an unspoken philosophy that creating a bill of rights could backfire on the government. Listing the specific rights that were going to be protected could encourage people to propose additional rights.

Chief Justice John Marshall is painted here. He served from 1801 to his death.

In the last essay, Hamilton asked readers if he did what he said he would do in the first essay—prove that the Constitution was a benefit to the nation. He reminded each man that reading and understanding this information was essential, as was making the right decision. He wrote:

Let us now pause and ask ourselves whether, in the course of these papers, the proposed Constitution has not been satisfactorily vindicated from the aspersions thrown upon it; and whether it has not been shown to be worthy of the public approbation and necessary to the public safety and prosperity. Every man is bound to answer these questions to himself, according to the best of his conscience and understanding, and to act agreeably to the genuine and sober dictates of his judgment. This is a duty

The People's Republic

The world at this time was full of monarchs. America was unique in being a republic. Monarchies in England and France operated on the idea that God, not the people, chose the king or queen. Therefore, this person was royal or higher than other people. This kind of thinking was completely rejected by the new Americans. They believed that the president should be a representative of the people and that we should democratically vote to decide who the "ruler" of the country will be. The president's position is not that of a dictator or tyrant and should not make decisions completely on their own. This is why the government needed to have a system of checks and balances. No one person should be in charge of an entire country.

Federalist Alexander Hamilton is shown here at his writing desk.

from which nothing can give him a dispensation. 'Tis the one he is called upon, nay, constrained by all the obligations that form the bands of society, to discharge sincerely and honestly.

Finally, the Federalists were done. For months their essays had appeared in various newspapers. Madison, Hamilton, and Jay had done what they had intended to do with those words. The people of the new nation had a better idea of what the Constitution might include and why it was written the way it was. Although that helped many people to make up their minds, there were still a great many who had some questions and objections. They were the people who had also kept up with the opposing opinions being published and found themselves agreeing with these viewpoints. These were the Anti-Federalists. They too had made reasonable and passionate arguments in this lengthy debate.

CHAPTER FIVE

THE ANTI-FEDERALIST ARGUMENT

As the Federalists were calling for a central authority, the Anti-Federalists were arguing against this much control. One aspect of their argument is that they fundamentally disagreed with the Federalists' view of human nature. The Federalists were greatly influenced by philosophers David Hume and John Locke. They believed that people, left with complete liberty, would become corrupt. The Anti-Federalists thought that people, even with almost complete freedom, would make reasoned decisions. Although the Anti-Federalists did not "win" the war of words, their arguments helped create a balanced constitution.

The Anti-Federalists

Led in part by Thomas Jefferson, the Anti-Federalists were made up of a variety of men. They all shared the concern that this new Constitution would give far too much power to the central government, instead of letting the individual states make most of the decisions. The Anti-Federalists rejected the idea of people looking to a huge, strong primary government for what

Philosopher David Hume is painted here. He lived from 1711 to 1776.

they needed. They believed in putting responsibility on the individual, not some glorious empire. Anti-Federalists trusted people to be decent and honest. They worried that the Federalists' image of government would eventually lead to tyranny and a never-ending desire for additional power. A central government would not have any real connection to the people, they argued. They worried that, under this new government, the president would become like the king they had just rejected. Similarly, they were concerned that the rich would be given more benefits than the poor, just as the big states would profit more than little ones. Anti-Federalists were also concerned that the Constitution contained no bill of rights. Many people had lost their lives and fought hard against England in the Revolutionary War to earn certain rights, so they wanted to make sure they kept them. Many of the essays the Anti-Federalists wrote focused on the lack of a bill of rights, and some of the states refused to agree to the ratification process without one. In 1791, one was created and added to the Constitution.

Founding Father George Washington led troops in the Revolutionary War when Americans rebelled against England.

Safety vs. Freedom

The differences between the two groups were actually simple. The Federalists believed that humans needed to be controlled. The Anti-Federalists felt they needed to be set free.

Unlike the Federalist Papers, which were written in an orderly fashion by three men, the Anti-Federalist essays were written by almost a dozen people and with far less organization. This hurt their movement and it is clear in looking back on the documents that they were on the losing side. They did not have the unified plans and actions their opponents did. The language used was slightly simpler, written more for working-class readers. An essay written under the pseudonym John DeWitt responded to the Federalists' attitude that adopting the Constitution would take care of all of the nation's problems. DeWitt wrote:

> We are told by some people, that upon the adopting [of] this New Government, we are to become the every thing in a Moment:—Our foreign and domestic debts will be as a Feather; our ports will be crowded

A Necessary Evil

In 1776, Thomas Paine wrote in his pamphlet, *Common Sense*, "Government, even in its best state, is but a necessary evil." Like Paine, many early Americans distrusted government. They knew they had to have one, but they wanted it to be as minimal as possible.

Many of the patriots who revolted against Britain also revolted against what they saw as an oppressive federal government. Patrick Henry was one of these patriots. His revolutionary spirit made him distrustful of any kind of government which seemed like a monarchy. He did not want the president of the United States to operate like a king and was hesitant to accept the Constitution. As Virginia governor in 1776 and then again in 1784, Henry helped to champion the Bill of Rights. The Bill of Rights is the first ten amendments to the Constitution and allowed individual liberties to be protected.

> with the ships of all the world, soliciting our commerce and our produce: Our manufacturers will increase and multiply; and, in short, if we STAND STILL, our country, notwithstanding, will be like the blessed Canaan, a land flowing with milk and honey. Let us not deceive ourselves; the only excellency of any government is in exact proportion to the administration of it:—Idleness and luxury will be as much a bane was ever: our passions will be equally at war with us then as now; and if we have men among us trying with all their ability to undermine our present Constitution, these very persons will direct their force to sap the vitals of the new one.

Call for Amendments

One of the primary ways that the Anti-Federalists battled the Constitution was by proposing a variety of amendments that they felt were necessary. Some were simple, while others were considered to be radical, especially those proposed by Rhode Island, the last state to agree to the Constitution. Rhode Island representatives strongly objected to the idea of keeping a standing army and wanted to ensure that Congress could not declare war without the approval of two-thirds of the senators and representatives.

Response of the Federal Farmer

One of the most outspoken Anti-Federalists was the so-called Federal Farmer. His essays have been considered some of the most eloquent and persuasive. In letters published in the *Poughkeepsie Country Journal*, he wrote about the possibility of slowing down and taking time to think things over carefully before making the decision to ratify the Constitution. Since the Federalists had repeatedly focused on safety issues in their essays, he decided to address the question from that perspective. He argued,

> If we remain cool and temperate, we are in no immediate danger of any commotions; we are in a state of perfect peace, and in no danger of invasions; the state governments are in the full exercise of their powers; and our governments will answer all present exigencies, except the regulation of trade, securing credit, in some cases, and providing for the interest, in some instances, of the public debts; and whether we adopt a change, three or nine months hence, can make but little odds with the private circumstances of individuals; their happiness and prosperity, after all, depend principally upon their own exertions.

One Great Republic?

Brutus was the main Anti-Federalist writer to work his way through the Constitution paragraph by paragraph, pointing out its problems and flaws in his essays. He urged readers to think about every element in the document and to consider whether they were truly necessary. He wrote:

> The first question that presents itself on the subject is, whether a confederated government be the best for the United States or not? Or in other words, whether the thirteen United States should be reduced to one great republic, governed by one legislature and under the direction of one executive and judicial; or whether they should continue thirteen confederated republics, under the direction and control of a supreme federal head for certain defined national purposes only?

Brutus also strongly disagreed with the idea of maintaining a permanent standing army. In one of his essays, he wrote:

> The liberties of a people are in danger from a large standing army, not only because the rulers may employ them for the purposes of supporting themselves in any usurpations of power, which they may see proper to exercise, but there is a great hazard, that an army will subvert the forms of the government, under whose authority they are raised, and establish one according to the pleasure of their leader.

Although some might look back at this time period and think that the Anti-Federalists were the "losers" in this lengthy debate, that is not really true. While the Constitution was eventually ratified, no group actually lost this historical argument. Instead, both sides made valid points that made the opposition think and even initiate some changes. Both parties made the

The United States Congress in the twenty-first century is photographed above. Many ideas of modern government are a result of the Federalist and Anti-Federalist debate.

people think about their beliefs, their wants, and their needs. Faced with the enormous challenge of trying to create a new country, everyone did their best to make the right decisions.

Current Debates

The debate over what should fall under states' rights and national government control did not end with the ratification of the Constitution. The issue pops up repeatedly in modern times, frequently between today's Republicans and Democrats. What is legally allowed in one state is sometimes not allowed in another. Whenever that happens, there is often discussion of letting the government take over the entire issue and make all the decisions. Recent issues that have been debated include same-sex marriages and homeschooling. Just like two hundred years ago, there are passionate, emotional, and intelligent people on either side of the issues, and while they may not officially debate through their local newspapers like the Federalists and Anti-Federalists did, their voices are heard one way or another.

More than two centuries after the Constitution was written, people still debate its contents. Occasionally, debates over constitutional issues lead to an amendment. Twenty-six amendments have been added since the Constitution was created. The last amendment was adopted in 1992. People of every political persuasion will most likely continue to strive to create that perfect union, difficult as it may be. Thanks to an impressive and dedicated group of Americans who took the time to write out their thoughts many years ago, people today have clearer ideas of what went into creating the nation's set of rules and regulations.

Perhaps George Washington summed it up best when he said, "The Federalist Papers have thrown a new light upon the science of government; they have given the rights of man a full and fair discussion and explained them in so clear and forcible a manner as cannot fail to make a lasting impression."

PRIMARY SOURCE TRANSCRIPTIONS

Federalist Essay No. 47: The Particular Structure of the New Government and the Distribution of Power Among Its Different Parts

From *The New-York Packet*, Friday, February 1, 1788.

To the People of the State of New York:

Having reviewed the general form of the proposed government and the general mass of power allotted to it, I proceed to examine the particular structure of this government, and the distribution of this mass of power among its constituent parts. One of the principal objections inculcated by the more respectable adversaries to the Constitution, is its supposed violation of the political maxim, that the legislative, executive, and judiciary departments ought to be separate and distinct. In the structure of the federal government, no regard, it is said, seems to have been paid to this essential precaution in favor of liberty. The several departments of power are distributed and blended in such a manner as at once to destroy all symmetry and beauty of form, and to expose some of the essential parts of the edifice to the danger of being crushed by the disproportionate weight of other parts. No political truth is certainly of greater intrinsic value, or is stamped with the authority of more enlightened patrons of liberty, than that on which the objection is founded.

The accumulation of all powers, legislative, executive, and judiciary, in the same hands, whether of one, a few, or many, and whether hereditary, self appointed, or elective, may justly be pronounced the very definition of tyranny. Were the federal Constitution, therefore, really chargeable with the accumulation of power, or with a mixture of powers, having a dangerous tendency to such an accumulation, no further arguments would be necessary to inspire a universal reprobation of the system. I persuade myself, however, that it will be made apparent to every one, that the charge cannot be supported, and that the maxim on which it relies has been totally misconceived and misapplied. In order to form correct ideas on this important subject, it will be proper to investigate the sense in which the preservation of liberty requires that the three great departments of power should be separate and distinct. The oracle who is always consulted and cited on this subject is the celebrated Montesquieu. If he be not the author of this invaluable precept in the science of politics, he has the merit at least of displaying and recommending it most effectually to the attention of mankind. Let us endeavor, in the first place, to ascertain his meaning on this point. The British Constitution was to Montesquieu what Homer has been to the didactic writers on epic poetry. As the latter have considered the work of the immortal bard as the perfect model from which the principles and rules of the epic art were to be drawn, and by which all similar works were to be judged, so this great political critic appears to have viewed the Constitution of England as the standard, or to use his own expression, as the mirror of political liberty; and to have delivered, in the form of elementary truths, the several characteristic principles of that particular system. That we may be sure, then, not to mistake his meaning in this case, let us recur to the source from which the maxim was drawn. On the slightest view of the British Constitution, we must perceive that the legislative, executive, and judiciary departments are by no means totally separate and distinct from each other. The executive magistrate forms an integral part of the legislative authority. He alone has the prerogative of making treaties with foreign sovereigns, which, when made, have, under certain limitations, the force of legislative acts. All the members of the judiciary department are appointed by him, can be removed by him on the address of the two Houses of Parliament, and form, when he pleases to consult them, one of his constitutional councils. One branch of the legislative department forms also a great constitutional council to the executive chief, as, on another hand, it is the sole depositary of judicial power in cases of impeachment, and is invested with the supreme appellate jurisdiction in all other cases. The judges, again, are so far connected with the legislative department as often to attend and participate in its deliberations, though not admitted to a legislative vote . . . The magistrate in whom the whole executive power resides cannot of himself make a law, though he can put a negative on every law; nor administer justice in person, though he has the appointment of those who do administer it. The judges can exercise no executive prerogative, though they are shoots from the executive stock; nor any legislative function, though they may be advised with by the legislative councils. The entire legislature can perform no judiciary act, though by the joint act of two of its branches the judges may be removed from their offices, and though one of its branches is possessed of the judicial power in the last resort. The entire legislature, again, can exercise no executive prerogative, though one of its branches constitutes the supreme executive magistracy, and another, on the impeachment of a third, can try and condemn all the subordinate officers in the executive department. The reasons on which Montesquieu grounds his maxim are a further demonstration of his meaning. "When the legislative and executive powers are united in the same person or body," says he, "there can be no liberty, because apprehensions may arise lest THE SAME monarch or senate should ENACT tyrannical laws to EXECUTE them in a tyrannical manner." Again: "Were the power of judging joined with the legislative, the life and liberty of the subject would be exposed to arbitrary control, for THE JUDGE would then be THE LEGISLATOR . . ."

PUBLIUS.

Anti-Federalist Essay No. 47: "Balance" of Departments Not Achieved

Under New Constitution

This essay is made up of excerpts from "Centinel's," letters of October 5 and 24, 1787. Taken from *The Independent Gazetteer*.

I am fearful that the principles of government inculcated in Mr. [John] Adams' treatise [Defence of the Constitutions of Government of the United States of America], and enforced in the numerous essays and paragraphs in the newspapers, have misled some well designing members of the late Convention.

But it will appear in the sequel, that the construction of the proposed plan of government is infinitely more extravagant.

I have been anxiously expecting that some enlightened patriot would, ere this, have taken up the pen to expose the futility, and counteract the baneful tendency of such principles. Mr. Adams' sine qua non [Latin: "without which, not"] of a good government is three balancing powers; whose repelling qualities are to produce an equilibrium of interests, and thereby promote the happiness of the whole community. He asserts that the administrators of every government, will ever be actuated by views of private interest and ambition, to the prejudice of the public good; that therefore the only effectual method to secure the rights of the people and promote their welfare, is to create an opposition of interests between the members of two distinct bodies, in the exercise of the powers of government, and balanced by those of a third. This hypothesis supposes human wisdom competent to the task of instituting three co-equal orders in government, and a corresponding weight in the community to enable them respectively to exercise their several parts, and whose views and interests should be so distinct as to prevent a coalition of any two of them for the destruction of the third. Mr. Adams, although he has traced the constitution of every form of government that ever existed, as far as history affords materials, has not been able to adduce a single instance of such a government. He indeed says that the British constitution is such in theory, but this is rather a confirmation that his principles are chimerical and not to be reduced to practice. If such an organization of power were practicable, how long would it continue? Not a day—for there is so great a disparity in the talents, wisdom and industry of mankind, that the scale would presently preponderate to one or the other body, and with every accession of power the means of further increase would be greatly extended. The state of society in England is much more favorable to such a scheme of government than that of America. There they have a powerful hereditary nobility, and real distinctions of rank and interests; but even there, for want of that perfect equality of power and distinction of interests in the three orders of government, they exist but in name. The only operative and efficient check upon the conduct of administration, is the sense of the people at large.

Suppose a government could be formed and supported on such principles, would it answer the great purposes of civil society? If the administrators of every government are actuated by views of private interest and ambition, how is the welfare and happiness of the community to be the result of such jarring adverse interests?

Therefore, as different orders in government will not produce the good of the whole, we must recur to other principles. I believe it will be found that the form of government, which holds those entrusted with power in the greatest responsibility to their constituents, the best calculated for freemen. A republican, or free government, can only exist where the body of the people are virtuous, and where property is pretty equally divided. In such a government the people are the sovereign and their sense or opinion is the criterion of every public measure. For when this ceases to be the case, the nature of the government is changed, and an aristocracy, monarchy or despotism will rise on its ruin. The highest responsibility is to be attained in a simple structure of government, for the great body of the people never steadily attend to the operations of government, and for want of due information are liable to be imposed on. If you complicate the plan by various orders, the people will be perplexed and divided in their sentiment about the source of abuses or misconduct; some will impute it to the senate, others to the house of representatives, and so on, that the interposition of the people may be rendered imperfect or perhaps wholly abortive. But if, imitating the constitution of Pennsylvania, you vest all the legislative power in one body of men (separating the executive and judicial) elected for a short period, and necessarily excluded by rotation from permanency, and guarded from precipitancy and surprise by delays imposed on its proceedings, you will create the most perfect responsibility. For then, whenever the people feel a grievance, they cannot mistake the authors, and will apply the remedy with certainty and effect, discarding them at the next election. This tie of responsibility will obviate all the dangers apprehended from a single legislature, and will the best secure the rights of the people . . .

This mixture of the legislative and executive moreover highly tends to corruption. The chief improvement in government, in modern times, has been the complete separation of the great distinctions of power; placing the legislative in different hands from those which hold the executive; and again severing the judicial part from the ordinary administrative. "When the legislative and executive powers (says Montesquieu) are united in the same person or in the same body of magistrates, there can be no liberty."

CENTINEL

CHRONOLOGY

1781 The Articles of Confederation go into effect.

1786 A convention meets in Annapolis, Maryland, to discuss the Articles of Confederation.

1787 The Constitutional Convention is held. The Federalist and Anti-Federalist essays begin to appear in various newspapers. The Constitution is drafted and approved; it is ratified by Delaware, Pennsylvania, and New Jersey.

1788 Federalist and Anti-Federalist essays continue to be published. Eight more states agree to ratify the Constitution.

1789 The Constitution takes effect. North Carolina ratifies the Constitution.

1790 Rhode Island ratifies the Constitution.

1791 The Bill of Rights is added to the Constitution.

GLOSSARY

anarchy A state of lawlessness.

bicameral Having two chambers or houses.

confederation A number of united parties or entities.

constitution A document that lists a series of rules or principles which a state or country adhere to.

drafted Written.

faction An individual group that gathers for political or economic interests.

judicial Relating to courts of law or to the administration of justice.

legislation A law or laws set by a government.

ordinance An authoritative command or order.

priggish Self-righteous; acting morally superior.

propagandistic Meant to persuade.

pseudonym A pen or pretend name used in publishing.

ratification The process of approving or agreeing to something officially.

republican A type of government which gives authority to the people to elect representatives and a president.

tyranny A government in which one person has all the power.

BIBLIOGRAPHY

Elkins, Stanley, and Eric McKitrick. *The Age of Federalism*. New York, NY: Oxford University Press, 1994.

Eze, Ugonna. "The Anti-Federalists and Their Important Role During the Ratification Fight." National Constitution Center. September 27, 2017. https://constitutioncenter.org/blog/the-anti-federalists-and-their-important-role-during-the-ratification-fight.

Ketcham, Ralph, ed. *The Anti-Federalist Papers and the Constitutional Convention Debates.* New York, NY: Signet, 2003.

Meisner, James Jr., and Amy Ruth. *American Revolutionaries and Founders of the Nation.* Springfield, NJ: Enslow Publishers, 1999.

Meyerson, Michael I.. *Liberty's Blueprint How Madison and Hamilton Wrote the Federalist Papers, Defined the Constitution, and Made Democracy Safe for the World*. New York, NY: Basic Books, 2009.

Old, Wendie C. *Thomas Jefferson (United States Presidents)*. Springfield, NJ: Enslow Publishers, 1997.

Rossiter, Clinton, ed. *The Federalist Papers*. New York, NY: Mentor, 1999.

White, Morton. *Philosophy, The Federalist, and the Constitution*. Oxford, UK: Oxford University Press, 1987.

Whitelaw, Nancy. *More Perfect Union: The Story of Alexander Hamilton (Notable Americans)*. Greensboro, NC: Morgan Reynolds, Inc., 1997.

FURTHER READING

Books

Duignan, Brian, and Carolyn DeCarlo. *The US Constitution and the Separation of Powers*. New York, NY: Britannica Educational Publishing, in Association with Rosen Educational Services, 2019.

Hamilton, Alexander, James Madison, and John Jay. *The Federalist*. Compiled by Robert A. Ferguson. New York, NY: Barnes and Noble Classics, 2006.

Hennessey, Jonathan, Justin Greenwood, and Brad Simpson. *Alexander Hamilton: The Graphic History of an American Founding Father*. New York, NY: Ten Speed Press, 2017.

Machajewski, Sarah. *Analyzing Sources of Information about the U.S. Constitution*. New York, NY: Rosen Publishing, 2018.

Merriman, Ben. *Conservative Innovators: How States Are Challenging Federal Power*. Chicago, IL: University of Chicago Press, 2019.

Websites

The Complete Federalist Papers

www.let.rug.nl/usa/documents/1786-1800/the-federalist-papers

Sponsored by the University of Groningen, this website has links to all of the Federalist Papers for free.

The Constitution Society

www.constitution.org

This site is a reference for deciding what is constitutional and what is not.

PBS Learning Media

ny.pbslearningmedia.org/resource/ham16.soc.ushis.federalist/hamiltons-america-the-federalist-papers

This website has videos and educational material that explains Hamilton's ideas and the Federalist Papers.

INDEX